Scenes from Georgia

MARGARET WILLES

The National Trust

The Print Room at Blickling Hall in Norfolk.

Introduction

Late Georgian country houses often contained Print Rooms. At Blickling Hall in Norfolk, for instance, Lord Buckinghamshire converted a bedroom into a Copperplate Room in 1793. Monochrome engravings of works by Old Masters such as Rubens and Claude, were pasted onto the walls with decorative borders, as though they were framed paintings. Other National Trust examples are to be found at Uppark in Sussex and The Vyne in Hampshire.

The Caricature Room at Calke Abbey in Derbyshire presents a very unusual variation on this theme. In place of engraved landscapes, views of buildings and other decorative

The Caricature Room at Calke Abbey in Derbyshire.

subjects, the room is filled with satirical cartoons of the late eighteenth and early nineteenth centuries. Many of the caricatures are by leading artists of the genre, including Thomas Rowlandson, James Gillray, George Cruikshank. In all, there are 148 on display, but conservators have found that there are more under the top layer, sometimes as many as three deep.

Exactly who created this room and when is not certain, but the dates of the caricatures provide us with some clues. The first prints date from the early 1790s, the latest from 1827, a fascinating period in the annals of the Harpur Crewe family of Calke. Sir Henry Harpur, the 7th Baronet, inherited Calke in 1789. Up to this time, the Harpurs had led the typical life of country-house gentry. They were rich, owners of considerable estates, devoted to horse-racing and country pursuits. Sir Henry was a Justice of the

Portrait of Sir George Crewe and his son John, by Ramsay Richard Reinagle, 1828.

Peace and served as High Sheriff of Derbyshire in 1794. During the Napoleonic Wars he raised a troop of yeomanry from his estates for the defence of the realm, commissioning Joseph Haydn to compose the *Derbyshire Marches* as appropriate music for the volunteers. Apart from the top-class musical commission, all this was par for the course.

But Sir Henry was not a man of convention. As soon as he inherited Calke, he withdrew from the usual contacts with society, and acquired as his mistress a lady's maid, Nanette Hawkins, with whom he lived in a small house in the park. In 1794 he amazed society by marrying Nanette, and retreated into the seclusion of Calke: he is known to posterity as the 'isolated baronet'. In this seclusion, he set about making various alterations to the layout of Calke Abbey. This included turning the ground-floor rooms in the south-east corner of the house into private family rooms or 'parlours' because they caught the sun and were close to the garden entrance. The Caricature Room is in this suite.

Sir Henry and Lady Harpur had eight children in all. Their eldest surviving son was George, born in 1795. He is the most likely candidate to have been responsible for acquiring the caricatures and pasting them on the walls. In the archives is one, tantalising reference; a schoolfriend, in an undated letter, wrote 'I shall bring no caricatures... how scurvily my last were used'.

George, however, scarcely spent much of his childhood at Calke. His journals, which begin in 1815, show that his father behaved as unconventionally towards him as towards the rest of the world. When he was at school at Rugby, the boy passed his holidays with Lady Skipwith at Newbold Hall in Warwickshire. Sir Henry would not countenance his son receiving an Oxbridge education, sending him instead to a private tutor, the Rev. Thomas Allsop at Fressingfield in Suffolk, as private and austere a man as Sir Henry. In a passage worthy of Dickens, George wrote in his journal on 25 November 1815 'O how do I long once again to embrace these dear Parents, whom now I have not seen for nearly two years.' He hoped to be asked to spend Christmas at Calke, but the invitation never came.

Sir Henry died suddenly in February 1819, in an extraordinary accident. Driving his phaeton, he had almost reached his destination in Hertfordshire when he accelerated the horses and drove against a post, falling to the ground and sustaining a fatal injury. His eldest son inherited as Sir George Crewe, and it is likely that the caricatures, which he may have been collecting over the years, were pasted onto the walls of the Caricature Room at Calke in the early 1820s, when he returned at last to his family home.

The term 'caricature' was first used in England in the 1750s: earlier generations referred to satires, derived from *satura*, a medley. These were applied to graphic pictorial renderings of the flow of events, moods and fashions. Apart from the *Cries of London,* most early eighteenth-century satires were political; artists had a field day with the scandal of the South Sea Bubble in 1720, for example. A few of the earliest caricatures were for private consumption, such as those by Lord Townshend, some of which are to be found in the collection at Felbrigg Hall in Norfolk.

As the century progressed, social themes began to proliferate. Favourites amongst these were sport, the theatre, connoisseurship, taste and fashion. Travel was very popular as it provided a splendid opportunity to have a dig at the French, Britain's constant enemy throughout the eighteenth century and the early years of the nineteenth. The social scene in London was also a fruitful target – the fashionable of St James's, coffee houses, taverns, shops and streets. These engravings, like the popular press today, enabled the country as a whole to find out what were the doings of the rich and famous, and to catch up on the latest trends.

Caricatures and other engravings could be purchased from print shops, where their prices ranged from sixpence (£1.40*) to a guinea (£59.50*) coloured for long strip designs. Some were aimed at collectors to be bound in portfolios for libraries, for applying to folding screens, such as the example that can be seen at Arlington Court in Devon, or for pasting on the walls, as at Calke Abbey. The cheaper end of the market was intended for display on street corners, in ale shops or for poorer households. Some prints were even hired out for evening entertainments.

The 1780s and 90s, and the first years of the nineteenth century are often described as the golden age of British caricatures, when Rowlandson and Gillray were at their peak. Their latest work was snapped up by gentlemen of leisure in London, whose morning routine might include a visit to a print shop such as Fores in Piccadilly, Holland in Oxford Street, Hannah Humphrey in Bond Street and later in St James's. Perhaps the most famous print seller was Rudolph Ackermann. He opened a school of drawing at 101 Strand in 1794, but closed it twelve years later and transferred his print-selling business there, employing refugees from France to colour the prints. He was also a publisher, and sold books alongside fancy articles and materials for artists. The coloured print borders in the Caricature Room at Calke were bought from Ackermann.

* As estimated in equivalent contemporary values of the pound compiled in 1999.

Detail of the early nineteenth-century scrap screen in the Staircase Hall at Arlington Court in Devon.

Although the Calke caricatures and engravings reflect the themes and fashions mentioned above, there are some interesting qualifications. The prints are almost entirely social in subject. Not all of them are satirical; some show soldiers resting on river banks or volunteers on the march, others are views of places, such as Chelsea Reach or the Pont Neuf in Paris. Relatively few have a strong political message, and particularly striking is the lack of satirical comment on the Royal Family. The goings on of the Prince of Wales and his disreputable brothers, which provided such wonderful opportunities for the artistic poison brush, particularly of Gillray, are completely absent. The sole example is a mild comment on the Duke of York's unfilial attitude (pages 40–1); ironically, he was regarded as one of George III's more devoted sons.

Sir George's journals do give us a few clues as to how his tastes and opinions might have dictated his choice of caricatures. Politically, he was a Conservative, adopted as their Parliamentary candidate for South Derbyshire in 1834, and duly winning the seat. This election came soon after the First Reform Bill, which had such a profound effect on the political scene in Britain. George reveals himself as moderate and rational in his views, considering that the House of Lords was showing lack of wisdom and foresight in trying to prevent parliamentary reform. The subject that caused him the most alarm was the prospect of violent revolution, which accords with the caricatures at Calke that warn of politics red in tooth and claw emanating from France at this period.

George's attitude towards the royal family would seem to have been respectful. When the Prince Regent at last succeeded to the throne in 1820, not everybody rejoiced, sickened by his many years of dissolute and selfish behaviour. But on 21 July 1821, George records a feast held to celebrate the coronation, with roast beef and plum pudding for the poor men of Ticknall, and medals for over 600 children.

George found London 'a hateful place, unless I had a comfortable, quiet house of my own, where I could be surrounded with my usual occupations'. He must, therefore, have enjoyed Rowlandson's portrayals of the miseries of living in the capital. Above all, he loved living at Calke with his beloved wife and growing family of children, providing such a contrast to the unconventional and erratic attitudes of his father.

I have chosen twenty-five images from Calke that reflect some of the aspects that I have outlined above. As the caricatures and prints have been on display for nearly two centuries, they have become faded, and quite often damaged, so that they are not of the same quality as examples kept in a portfolio. This is shown to dramatic effect when the *Pic-Nic Orchestra* is reproduced alongside a companion image, *Dilettanti Theatricals* from the collection at Wimpole Hall (p.31). But the Calke images provide a fascinating glimpse of Georgian life, telling us so much of the interests and obsessions, prejudices and curiosities of the time. Many of these same subjects, moreover, are capable of exciting similar passions today.

I am indebted to David Crawford and Islay Sayles for their research into the cartoons, and their reproduction of information from Frederick Stephens and M. Dorothy George's *British Museum's Catalogue of Political and Personal Satires*, compiled between 1870 and 1954, and Joseph Grego's *Rowlandson the Caricaturist*. I have also found invaluable Dorothy George's *Hogarth to Cruikshank: Social Change in Graphic Satire*, and Christopher Hibbert and Ben Weinreb's *London Encyclopaedia*. Insight into the life of Sir George has been provided by *Squire of Calke Abbey: The Journals of Sir George Crewe 1815–34*, edited by Colin Kitching. Thank you too to Alastair Laing, the Trust's Advisor on Paintings and Maggie Gowan, Manager of the Photographic Library, who had the idea in the first place.

Margaret Willes
September 2000

A Follower of Fashion

A Crop, of 1791

Artist: I. Cruickshaks*
Published September 1791 by
S.H.* Fores, 3 Piccadilly

This dashing figure is wearing the very latest in men's fashion of the period: short top-boots, tight-fitting breeches or pantaloons, a waistcoat with a high collar, a coat slipping off his shoulder, and a high crowned hat. His hair is cut very short, hence the term 'crop'.

Sir Nathaniel Wraxall, writing in 1815, attributed this new style to the revolutionary turbulence in France: '...dress never fell till the era of Jacobinism and equality in 1793 and 1794. It was then that pantaloons, cropped hair and shoe strings, as well as the total abolition of buckles and ruffles, together with the disuse of hair-powder characterised the men.' This revolution in dress can be seen by comparing the 'Crop' with the 'ancien regime', two examples of Macaronis as satirised by H.W. Bunbury in 1772 (one of which is shown

* Isaac Cruikshank was a well-known caricaturist and father of George. The incorrect spelling, together with the change in the publisher's second initial (it should be 'W') suggests that this is an example of passing-off by a pirate imitator.

The St James's Macaroni
by H. Bunbury, 1772,
published by J. Brotherton,
134 New Bond Street.

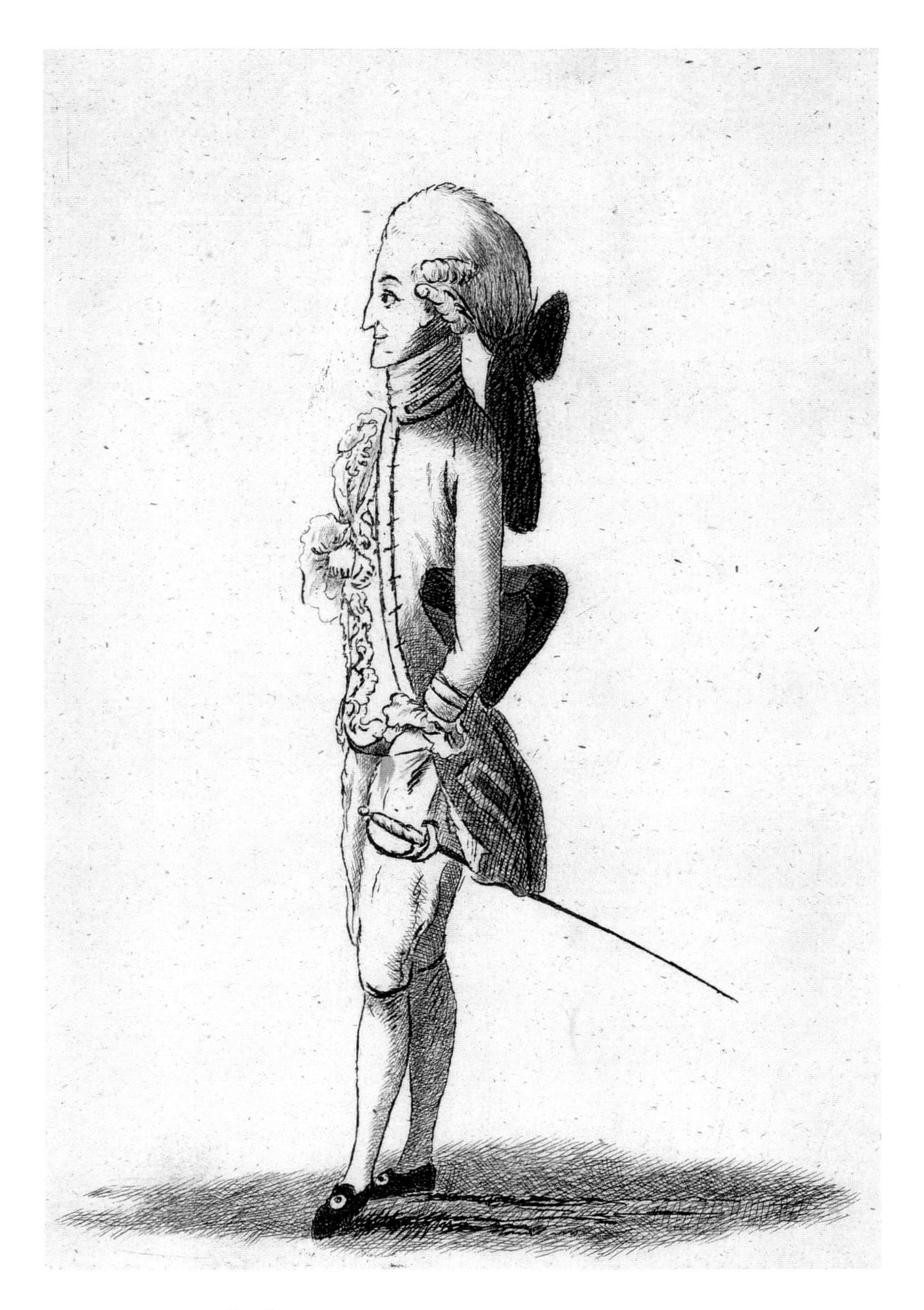

right, the other on the title page), from the Windham collection at Felbrigg Hall in Norfolk. Macaronis were young aristocrats from the fashionable quarters of St James's, and their imitators, who assumed exaggerated manners and gait. Their dress was characterised by a close-fitting frock coat and waistcoat, and they often sported a sword as a decorative accessory alongside a huge nosegay.

Our fashionable Crop, on the other hand, may have retained the affected gait, but he carries an uncompromising bludgeon, and looks through his eye-glass with a sneer. The likely subject of this engraving is Lord Barrymore, or one of his brothers. Boon companions of George, the Prince of Wales, they were known as wild rakes in London Society.

The Perils of Fashion: Ice

A Naked Truth, or Nipping Frost

Artist: George Cruikshank
Published 2 February 1803 by S.W. Fores, 50 Piccadilly

The fashions for ladies' dress also came from France, and again represented a revolution in style. Gone were the huge hoops and wide skirts – confined to court levées at St James's Palace, where Queen Charlotte held on to this exercise in formal grandeur until her death in 1818. Instead, fashionable ladies adopted clinging, muslin robes that revealed their figures, much to the outrage of the media. The *Sporting Magazine* in 1794 fulminated 'Female dress of the present fashion is perhaps the most indecent ever seen in this country. The breast is altogether displayed, and the whole drapery, by the wanton management of the wearers...is said to cling so to the figure that nothing can be said to be completely concealed. Well may it be necessary to veil the face.'

Legend has it that young ladies would lie in cold baths to achieve the clinging look and that some caught their deaths as a result, but this is probably like many old wives' tales – more famous in the telling. Nevertheless, the light muslins from India were not very suitable for winter socialising. In a letter to her sister Cassandra dated 8 January 1803, Jane Austen describes a dinner party in Hampshire, where 'Mrs Powlett was at once expensively and nakedly dressed; we have had the satisfaction of estimating her Lace and Muslin'.

To get some warmth, ladies carried fur muffs and wore 'a bosom friend', a tippet to protect the throat and chest, or a short tailored jacket called a spencer, after the 2nd Earl Spencer. These can be seen in Cruikshank's etching, contrasting with the dress of the coachman, well wrapped in his many-caped greatcoat.

GSC invt
TRUTH, or NIPPING FROST
ccadilly
Folios of Caracatures lent out for the Evening
Yet Jack sorely nip'd, and pinch'd, her bare bum,
She wriggl'd and wreath and shew'h many strange whim
But Dolly poor girl, lost the use of her Limbs,
Paid dear for the Fashion, her Folly and Pride,
Went home to her bed and there lingering died,
Then Ladies, beware lest Jack Frost should obtrude,
Your nakedness cover, he's apt to be rude.

Perils of Fashion: Fire

Advantages of wearing Muslin Dresses

Artist: James Gillray
Published 15 February 1802 by H. Humphrey, 27 St James's Street

Gillray depicts the hazards of fire. Chaos ensues when a red-hot poker falls out of the fire onto the muslin dress of a hostess as she presides over the tea-table. The scalding contents of the urn and teapot, and a picture of Vesuvius in eruption on the chimneypiece all add to the heat of the moment.

Fire has always presented a danger to women wearing long skirts, and servants working with open fires in the kitchens were particularly vulnerable. Muslin, a form of light cotton woven in India, caught fire terribly easily. In the mid-nineteenth century the French ballerina Emma Livry was burnt to death when her muslin tutu was set alight during a rehearsal; ironically she was playing a butterfly that flies too close to a flame.

In this cartoon Gillray is also showing another peril of the Empire line – its unsuitability for the fuller figure. The simple dresses were intended to look like classical drapery. The *Ladies Monthly Magazine* for March 1803, for instance, pointed out that had 'a party of high-bred young ladies who were dressed or rather undressed in all the nakedness of the mode...been placed on pedestals or niched in recesses, they might have passed for so many statues very lightly shaded with drapery'. Unfortunately many of those who adopted the fashion were not of these proportions, and looked monstrous as a consequence. One of Gillray's favourite targets was Albinia Bertie, wife of the 3rd Earl of Buckinghamshire, a member of the Pic-Nic Society (see pages 30–1).

A Windswept Girl in a Turban by Arthur William Devis, painted in the late 1780s. This portrait shows how the light-weight muslin flattered the slender figure.

Thus we'll Join Heads & Hands all discord shall cease,
And with Bottles & Glasses the Union increase.
The UNION CLUB.
As
And to

Celebrating the Union

The Union Club

Artist: Charles Williams
Published 8 February 1801 by S.W. Fores, 50 Piccadilly

This is one of the few caricatures at Calke that deals with politics. It is an imitation by Charles Williams of a famous engraving of the same name by James Gillray, and refers to the Union Club which was founded in 1799 'when the Union of the Parliament of England and Ireland was in agitation'. The Club's original home was at Cumberland House, Pall Mall, and among early members were Charles James Fox and the playwright, Richard Brinsley Sheridan. William Pitt the Younger succeeded in bringing about the political union of the two countries, and on 1 January 1801, the first joint parliament of England and Ireland was summoned. His triumph, however was short-lived, as Pitt linked with the union the emancipation of Roman Catholics, and this was bitterly opposed by the King: Pitt resigned two months later.

Gillray based his print on a party held on 19 January to celebrate the birthday of Queen Charlotte, but developed the conviviality into scenes of debauchery and mayhem that reflect the complicated reactions of various politicians to the union. Williams followed suit with his satire. Pitt in a green jacket is shown pouring wine for the Duke of Newcastle. Fox is on the extreme right, asleep on two chairs. The chair of state is decorated with three hands joined in union (a parody of the device of the Order of the Bath, *tria juncta in una*), enclosed in a circle formed by a snake, emblem of Eternity. The pillars of the canopy are garlanded with thistles (Scotland), roses (England) and shamrock (Ireland). The top of the chairback is a cap of Liberty with two crossed axes: from this hangs the plumed cap of the Prince of Wales. The Prince himself cannot be seen, but probably his legs are below Fox's chairs. Sheridan sits on the far right, glass in hand, pipe in the other. The stately Cholmondeley, one of the Pic-Nickers (see pages 30–1), is shown embracing the lawyer, Sir James Erskine.

Williams' caricature appeared only two weeks after Gillray's, and was probably commissioned by his publisher to prevent the market being totally scooped by his rival, Hannah Humphrey.

Cries of London

No. 5: Water Cresses, come buy my Water Cresses

Artist: Thomas Rowlandson
Published 1 March 1799 at
R. Ackermann's, 101 Strand

Street cries were an old London tradition, first mentioned in the fourteenth century in William Langland's *Piers Plowman*. Foodstuffs, from hot pies to spices and fat chickens, were carried and cried by a huge range of sellers. Non-food products included small coal and second-hand clothes. In *Persuasion*, Jane Austen has her heroine speaking of the noise on the streets of Bath: 'bawlings of newsmen, muffin-men and milkmen'. Today the tumult of street markets and the rare cries of the rag and bone man and the newspaper vendor are our only reminders.

The first illustrations of London Cries came in 1687, when Marcellus Lauron portrayed seventy-four subjects that were engraved by Pierre Tempest. These proved steady sellers for the next two hundred years. In the 1790s Francis Wheatley produced *The Itinerant Trades of London*, and Thomas

No. 8: Hot cross Bunns two a penny Bunns

Artist: Thomas Rowlandson
Published 4 May 1799 at
R. Ackermann's, 101 Strand

Rowlandson responded with *Cries of London* published in 1799. In the watercress seller, an old man knocks at the door of Mrs Burke's establishment in Portland Street – probably a brothel, judging from the ladies who hang out of the window above. He is accosted by a young, hardworking mother and her child assistant. Cress sellers were usually the first on the morning streets, and their watercress may have some connotations of purity, contrasting with the late night activities of the brothel.

In the hot cross bun seller, a mother and her children are buying buns from a respectable working woman. The indulgence of giving buns to the children contrasts with the uncharitable gesture of a fat, bewigged clerical dignitary, shown in the background, sweeping aside an appeal for alms. Clerical hypocrisy was a favourite topic of Georgian caricaturists.

Cries of London

No. 4: Do you want any brick-dust

Artist: Thomas Rowlandson
Published 20 February 1799 at
R. Ackermann's, 101 Strand

Two more subjects from Rowlandson's series. Brick-dust was sold like sand, acting as a cleaning agent for floors and stairs where it could soak up grease and mud. It was also used for scouring metal, especially steel and brass.

The young housemaid is shown receiving not only the brick-dust, but also the leering attention of the seller. The interaction between the sexes is as important to Rowlandson as the subject matter: the pretty girl, the lecherous male, the censorious old woman. In the background, a sweep's brush sticks out of a chimney pot, and a couple flirt from attic windows.

Dust was a component of Georgian city recycling. The brick-making industry consumed large quantities of coal ash and cinders. Sweepers who collected and sold the dust were among the shadowy community inhabiting the brick

No. 6: All a growing, a growing; here's Flowers for your Gardens

Artist: Thomas Rowlandson
Published 1 March 1799 at
R. Ackermann's, 101 Strand

and cinder yards, and the laystalls (rubbish tips) that fringed the rapidly expanding metropolis, so hauntingly described by Charles Dickens in *Our Mutual Friend*. They may have been poor, but they regarded their livelihood as a lucrative business to be protected, and when Henry Mayhew was compiling his *London Labour and the London Poor* in 1861, he found that the occupation was hereditary.

The smart young gardener offering his pots of flowers and plants to the pretty young lady, provides Rowlandson with another opportunity to imply amorous intent. There were no florist's shops as such in eighteenth-century London; mixed flowers in bunches were sold in street markets or by vendors. Plant sellers, often nurserymen, would bring their plants into the centre of cities on donkey carts, with special staging.

England Expects...

Private Drilling, No. 5 in series

Artist: Thomas Rowlandson
Published 1 August 1798 at Ackermann's Gallery, 101 Strand

A favourite target for eighteenth-century caricaturists were 'Cits', London citizens from rich aldermen to shop-keepers. They would be portrayed at city feasts, shooting and fishing, visiting the pleasure gardens at Ranelagh or Vauxhall to rub shoulders with the fashionable, on Sunday outings, or taking holidays by the seaside.

In this series by Rowlandson, a fat 'Cit' is being drilled in his shop by an officer and a drummer boy, while his family watch in admiration. In the background are jars of snuff.

Trained bands had protected the City from civil unrest since Tudor times. In June 1780, the London Trained Bands and the Honourable Artillery Company, with whom they were affiliated, were called out during the Gordon Riots. Fifty thousand protesters, organised by the young MP Lord George Gordon, marched from Southwark to Parliament with a petition against the Catholic Relief Act, which intended to remove some of the penal laws against Roman Catholics. But Gordon lost control of the crowd, and burning and looting ensued. The City, regretting its initial softly-softly approach, brought out the militia and regular troops to restore order. As a result of this experience, the trained bands were reorganised in 1794 as the City of London Militia.

The 'Cit' would also be expected to act as a kind of home guard, able to take up arms when England was in danger of invasion. When Rowlandson produced this aquatint, Britain had been at war with France for five years. Apart from one brief interlude between March 1802 and March 1803, this conflict was to continue until 1815 and the defeat of Napoleon at Waterloo.

Paris Rappe
47
RAPPEE
BRAZIL
IRISH

Scientific Experiment

Experimental Philosophy, or Circulation

Artist: L. Foy
Published by W. Holland, 50 Oxford Street

The subjects of magnetism and electricity were highly fashionable in the late eighteenth century, attracting some very colourful and dubious characters. One such was the mystic Katterfelto who, with his black cats, gave lectures on the 'Philosophical, Mathematical, Optical, Magnetical, Electrical, Physical, Chemical, Pneumatic, Hydraulic, Hydrostatic, Proetic, Stenographic, Blaencical, and Caprimantic Arts'.

Another was James Graham, a doctor from Scotland, expert on 'Meico-Electrical Apparatus'. He established a Temple of Health and Hymen first in Adelphi Terrace, and later at Schomberg House in Pall Mall. With the help of 'nymphs', one of whom was Emma Hart, later to be Emma

Hamilton, mistress of Admiral Nelson, he unveiled his Grand Celestial Bed. This had a dome lined with mirrors, coloured sheets and a mattress 'filled with strongest, most springy hair, produced at vast expense from the tails of English stallions'. Patients could hire the bed for £50 per night to conceive perfect babies as 'even the barren must do when so powerfully agitated in the delights of love'.

Less exciting but very fashionable was the belief that mild shocks from static electricity could improve the health. The 2nd Earl of Buckinghamshire installed a Physic Closet in his house at Blickling; in 1793 an apparatus 'for electrifying' was recorded there. In this print, a family party discovers that an electric shock may be passed along a line of people, starting from the electrostatic source on the right-hand side. The cats on the lap of the lady in the armchair leap into the air, causing the gout sufferer to fling his crutch and demolish the tea tray brought in by the servant.

The Country Fair

Doctor Botherum, the Mountebank

Artist: Thomas Rowlandson
Published 6 March 1800

The credulity of country folk was a familiar theme for caricaturists, though city types were equally gullible when it came to mountebanks like Dr Botherum. During fair-time, agricultural workers would flock into their local market town, and enjoy the attractions and services on offer.

In the centre of this scene, Dr Botherum, dressed in fine court costume, is telling the crowd of his nostrums and elixirs to heal all manner of ailments. He is aided in this performance by his attendants, Merry Andrew and Jack Pudding. To his left, a third assistant is drawing teeth. Although he has transposed the scene to a country town, Rowlandson may have based his mountebank on Dr Bossy, a German 'respectable' charlatan who would arrive at his pitch in Covent Garden Market in London dressed in gold-laced coat, and drawn in a chariot attended by liveried servants. Lady Mary Wortley Montagu was baffled by the incredulity of the English in matters medical, 'As we no longer trust in miracles and relics, we run as eagerly after receipts and doctors, and the money which was given three centuries ago for the health of the soul, is now given for the health of the body...Quacks are despised in countries where they have shrines and images'.

Botherum may enjoy centre stage, but Rowlandson has filled the scene with mini-dramas. On the left, 'street food' is being eagerly consumed. In the centre, a portly butcher and a slipshod tailor quarrel for the attentions of a young lady. On the right, a Jewish pedlar is offering a potential customer items of haberdashery from his pack.

Exquisite Terror

Tales of Wonder!

Artist: James Gillray
Published 1 February 1802 by H. Humphrey,
27 St James's Street

Gillray is here poking fun at the literary vogue for melodrama and Gothic horror. The real *Tales of Wonder* were a harmless anthology to which Sir Walter Scott contributed a ballad, but the caricature is dedicated to Matthew Gregory Lewis, whose novel *The Monk* was published in 1796 after he narrowly escaped prosecution for indecency. The monk in question was Ambrosio, a worthy superior of the Capuchin order in Madrid. Falling to the temptations of a fiend-inspired woman disguised as a boy in his monastery, he is so depraved that he pursues one of his penitents and kills her to avoid detection. The book ends with him being hurled to destruction and damnation by the Devil. So popular did the book prove that thereafter the author was known as 'Monk' Lewis.

Four ladies are shown around the drawing-room table; one reads from a first edition of *The Monk*, while the others listen with rapt terror. Behind them a picture shows a girl being carried off to rape and slaughter, while the ornaments on the chimneypiece reflect the horror.

This taste for the supernatural and the terrible was also mocked by Jane Austen in *Northanger Abbey*, which she wrote in 1798, though it was not published until after her death in 1818. Her particular target was Mrs Radcliffe's *The Mysteries of Udolpho* (1794), in which the heroine is carried off by her aunt's villainous husband to a remote castle in the Apennines, where life, honour and fortune are threatened and she is surrounded by apparently supernatural terrors.

The MONK

A Question of Taste

Taste

Artist: Thomas Rowlandson (?)
Published 2 April 1801 by R. Ackermann, 101 Strand

Connoisseurs of art were favourite subjects for satirists, who liked to mock their pretensions, and to suggest that interest in classical figures masked a taste for the pornographic. In 1794 James Gillray made a drawing of one of the most famous connoisseurs of the time, Richard Payne Knight, in which he is shown examining a piece of classical *virtú*, which he endows with an upright member through the inadvertent placing of his thumb. Knight was a leading figure of the Dilettanti Society, and sat on the parliamentary committee for public monuments, known as the Committee of Taste.

The connoisseur shown in this caricature is not quite in the same league. He is asking his neighbour Jenkins, 'What do you think of my new purchase? – there's Taste for you. Mr Bronze bought it for me. I think he calls it a Chinese Goss or Joss or something like that – what a fine grim countenance, and do you mind the Higgle-de-griphicks stuck all about him. Something very deep and learned in that, I dare say, if one coud but make it out – I'll have him put up in the lawn, plump facing the road D–m me how the stage coach passengers will stare – I should not wonder if it was to frighten some of the fellows off the Roof.' The combination of a Chinese figure with hieroglyphics mingles memories of the objects brought back from China by Lord Macartney's embassy in 1794 with more recent Egyptian items, which came to England after Napoleon's defeat in the Battle of the Nile in 1798.

The *nouveau riche* had got in on the connoisseur act, much to the disapproval of those who considered themselves arbiters of taste. Lady Pembroke wrote in 1779 'There being a fashion for antiques now in England is quite a mistake. They are admired according to their desert as usual by those who understand them'. The foundation of the Royal Academy under George III's patronage had, according to some, made the taste for *virtú* universal, 'persons of all ranks and degrees set up for connoisseurs, and even the lowest people tell familiarity of Hannibal Scratchi, Paul Varnish and Raphael Angelo.'

There Neighbour Jenkins, what do you think of my new purchase — Theres Taste for you
Mr Bronze bought it for me — I think he calls it a Chinese Gofs or Jofs or something like
that — what a fine grim countenance, and do you mind the Higgle-de-griphicks — stuck
all about him, something very deep and larned in that, I dare say, if one coud but make
it out — I'll have him put up in the lawn, plump facing the road — D—n me how the stage
coach pafsengers will stare — I should not wonder if it was to frighten some of the fellows
off the Roof!

PICNIC
CONCERT
Imitations
Nightingale
by Lord C.
Tom Tit
Lord M.E.
Jackdaw
Genl. G.
Screech Owl
Lady B.

The Pic-Nic Society

The Pic-Nic Orchestra

Artist: James Gillray
Published 23 April 1802 by H. Humphrey, St James's Street

The Pic-Nic Society was formed by a group of aristocrats who adopted the French fashion for bringing their own food and drink to their formal entertainments. To prevent unfairness and meanness, tickets were drawn to find out who should provide what. One of the leading lights was Albinia, Countess of Buckinghamshire, described as 'the biggest and most dazzling star in the hemisphere of fashion'; another was Lt-Col Henry Francis Greville (a remote relative of George Crewe), who organised public performances in a little theatre in Tottenham Court Road.

Their apparently harmless activities sparked off a pamphlet war. This was fuelled by the playwright, Richard Brinsley Sheridan, who accused them of infringing the monopoly of Patent Theatres and threatened them with proceedings for vagrancy. Sheridan proved triumphant, and their enterprise collapsed.

The Orchestra consists of the enormous form of Lady Buckinghamshire at the piano. Behind her are the contrasting figures of Lord Cholmondeley playing the flute, and the diminutive Viscount Valletort at the cello. On the right, Colonel Greville plays the violin, and Lady Salisbury the horn, a reference to her sporting activities.

Dilettanti Theatricals – or – A Peep at the Green Room by Gillray, 1803.

A companion caricature, from the collection at Wimpole Hall in Cambridgeshire, shows the Pic-Nics indulging in Dilettanti Theatricals (above). Lady Buckinghamshire, vast in her muslin dress, repairs her make-up and learns her part. The spirited Lady Salisbury pulls on huntsman's breeches and boots, while her husband plays the fiddle. The huge figure on the throne is Lord Cholmondeley, wearing a sash inscribed *Amor vincit omnia*, a reference to his amorous proclivities. In the background, the Prince of Wales dances with his mistress, Lady Jersey, and his secret wife, Mrs Fitzherbert.

Exchange Alley

Lloyd's Coffee House

Artist: George Woodward
Published in 1798

Coffee houses were introduced to England in the mid-seventeenth century. The first in London, Pasqua Rosee's Head, was opened in 1652 by a Turkey merchant, Daniel Edwards, in St Michael's Alley, Cornhill. He offered the 'strong, bitter brew' lately imported from the Middle East. The idea took off, and by 1740 there were over 500 houses in the City, serving the exotic combination of Turkish coffee, West Indian sugar, Chinese tea and Virginian tobacco.

These houses were like clubs, where men (and only men) of similar mind could meet. In Pall Mall, Tories frequented the Cocoa Tree, while the Whigs favoured St James's. The theatrical scene gathered at Bedford Coffee House in the piazza at Covent Garden. William Hogarth's father opened an establishment in Smithfield which was learned and literary in tone, advertising for songs or poems that were 'New and Entertaining' to be left at his house: an idea that never got off the ground. Edward Lloyd was much luckier – or shrewder – with his coffee house first opened in 1692 on the corner of Abchurch and Lombard Streets. It quickly became known as the place where ship's captains, shipowners and merchants congregated and exchanged trustworthy shipping news.

By the time Woodward made this print, coffee houses were on the decline. The lure of coffee at twopence a cup, a pipe of tobacco at a penny and free newspapers had palled before the delights of men's clubs for the select and taverns and public houses for lesser mortals. But Edward Lloyd's Coffee House had developed into two great City institutions, Lloyds Register of Shipping, which was fully established in the 1760s, and Lloyds of London, which moved to the Royal Exchange in 1771.

Morning Chronic

The Sights of London

The Horse Armoury in the Tower

Artist: Unknown – Thomas Rowlandson?
Published 1808 by R. Ackermann, Repository of Arts, 101 Strand
Probably produced but never used for *The Microcosm of London*, which was illustrated by Pugin and Rowlandson

A group of sightseers are being shown around the Horse Armoury by a yeoman of the guard. In the seventeenth century, Charles II had concentrated the royal collection here to provide a showplace of armour and weapons associated with the history of England. Famous figures, such as Charles I, his elder brother, Henry Prince of Wales, and his favourite, the Duke of Buckingham, astride their horses provided one of the major tourist attractions of Georgian London. Another was the royal menagerie of exotic beasts introduced to the Tower of London by Henry III, and kept in the Lion Tower until moved to the Zoological Gardens in Regent's Park in 1838. The inmates of the menagerie in 1828 were recorded as 'a grizzly bear, an elephant, and one or two birds'.

The visitors are a far cry from the 'polite tourists' who had the money, leisure and status to gain access to Tudor palaces and great private houses and gardens in earlier times. Here we see two soldiers, one with his sweetheart, and two countrymen up for the market. Yet they represent the vanguard of future tourism. As the Tower ceased to play its political role as a prison and place of execution, so it became history as epitomised in Harrison Ainsworth's romantic novel, *The Tower of London*, illustrated by George Cruikshank and published in 1840. But the book was not just romance; Ainsworth also wanted to describe the parts of the Tower not open to the general public, and to point out how neglected the buildings were becoming. In October 1841, his warnings were justified when the Tower suffered a severe fire that completely destroyed the Horse Armoury. At Christmas that year, 3,000 people came to visit the ruins, and the numbers have been growing ever since.

TRUMP
GOLD BEATER
Rowlandson inv
MISERIES OF LONDON.
In going out to dinner (already too late) your carriage delayed by a jam of coaches — which choak up t
least an hour or more than you require: to sharpen your wits for table talk! —
" Breast against breast with ruinous assault
" And deafning shock they come —
Pub

Miseries of London: Traffic

Miseries of London: in going out to dinner ...

Artist: Thomas Rowlandson
Published 1 February 1807 by R. Ackeman [sic], 101 Strand

This caricature is one of a series by Rowlandson to illustrate *Miseries of Human Life* published by Ackermann. It shows a dinner guest, already late, getting stuck in a traffic jam of coaches and carriages.

The streets of London have always been packed with people. In the 1670s John Oldham wrote a poem listing the reasons for not living in London. He complained:

> While tides of followers behind you throng
> And, pressing on your heels, shove you along
> One with a board, or rafter, hits your head
> Another with his elbow bores your side

As Rowlandson graphically shows us, road rage is not a modern phenomenon. The Thames provided a useful highway, but as the metropolis expanded and grew away from the river, so the main routes became congested. The roads leading onto London Bridge were too narrow, while the east–west routes suffered from chronic bottlenecks, such as St Giles's High Street for Oxford Street and High Holborn, and the valley of the Fleet River for the Strand and Fleet Street.

Another hazard was dirt and rubbish. The City authorities tried to keep their streets clean and unobstructed, getting householders to contribute towards paving, lighting and rubbish collection. Westminster lagged behind until 1762, when a Paving Act established that slabs of granite should be laid on the roads, with raised pavements to separate pedestrians and vehicles. Rubbish was supposed to be collected by 'Rakers' in covered carts, but as Jonas Hanway reported in 1754: 'The Rakers not only drop near a quarter of their dirt and render a whole street, perhaps already cleansed, in many spots very filthy, but it subjects every coach and every passenger, of what quality whatsoever, to be overwhelmed with whole cakes of dirt at every accidental jolt of the cart'.

Every effort to improve led to increased traffic, made worse in the early nineteenth century, when gas and water companies were constantly digging up the roads to lay their pipes. The new Mayor of London is facing a familiar situation.

Miseries of London: Babies

Miseries of Social Life: After dinner when the cloth has been removed ...

Artist and publisher, Thomas Rowlandson,
9 April 1807, 1 James Street, Adelphi

Thomas Rowlandson continues his tale of woe by showing the hazards of dining out once the guest has got to his destination.

François de la Rochefoucauld, who visited England in 1784, observed that guests would travel over bad roads to dinner parties 'though they own to being bruised to death and quite deshabillered by jolts'. He was horrified by the length of time spent at the table, 'Dinner is one of the most wearisome of English experiences, lasting as it does four or five hours.' At this time the fashionable hour for dining was 7pm, with men and women sitting alternately in what one commentator described as 'a new promiscuous mode of seating'. Segregation had prevailed in earlier times, but this method enabled ladies to be helped to the food by their neighbour.

Formal dinners were divided into two or occasionally three courses, each consisting of a variety of dishes, including sweet puddings. After these, the cloth would be removed and the dessert served, baskets of fresh and candied fruit, sweetmeats, jellies, ices and syllabubs. In Rowlandson's caricature, the moment has come when 'the wine of conversation as well as the bottle is just beginning to brighten'. But to the horror of the guest, his anticipation of the delights to come are ruined by the arrival of the nursemaids with the many children of the household: 'A string of staring babies brought in and carried round to be caressed and admired during the rest of the sitting....' As in *Tales of Wonder* (pp. 26–7), the paintings and the porcelain on the chimneypiece reflect the theme of babies.

La Rochefoucauld would have sympathised with the guest's reaction, for he liked the British habit of lingering at table while the ladies retired to tea in the drawing-room. 'Conversation is as free as it can be, everyone expresses his political opinions with much frankness. Sometimes conversation becomes extremely free upon highly indecent topics...very often I have heard things mentioned in good society which would be in the grossest taste in France.'

MISERIES OF SOCIAL LIFE.

n removed and the wine of conversation as well as the bottle is just beginning to brighten — seeing the door open and a string of stari
nd admired during the rest of the sitting — an Outrage from which there is not even a bye law or dead letter statute under our otherwise
edress.

Pub April 9 1807 by T Rowlandson N 1 James St Adelphi

Royal Scandals

Making most of £10,000 Per Ann[um] by saving travelling expences

Artist: Unsigned, but probably by J.L. Marks,
who produced a very similar caricature that he also published.
This may, therefore, be a pirated edition.
Published 1819 by Sidebethem, 287 Strand

The family of George III and his consort, Charlotte of Mecklenburg-Strelitz provided a wonderful source for the caricaturists, so it is strange that this is the only example at Calke specifically concerned with the activities of the Royals. It is, moreover, a very mild satire compared to some, which have never been equalled in their unmitigated venom.

This caricature shows Frederick, Duke of York, second son of George and Charlotte, who was born in 1763 and died in 1827. He is depicted riding a velocipede, also known as a pedestrian hobby horse, dandy hobby or accelerator. This eccentric means of transport was introduced in 1818 from France, where it had been patented by Karl von Drais, and in 1819 it was the subject for satirical prints. Dandies were associated with velocipedes, though surely they never actually rode one?

Parodied as the 'Grand Old Duke of York' while commanding the British army in the Netherlands in 1794, Frederick was an adequate but not very inspiring soldier. In 1809 he was accused of corrupt practices, allowing his mistress, Mary Ann Clarke, to sell army commissions, and the resulting enquiry revealed scurrilous details of his relationship with Mrs Clarke. His older brother, George, Prince of Wales, was only too pleased to see the spotlight move from his own scandalous conduct, and Frederick was obliged to resign, greatly upsetting the King.

Ten years later, George III's insanity made him a recluse in Windsor Castle, with Prince George acting as Regent. On the Queen's death in 1818 the Prince Regent invited his brother to undertake the office of *Custos Personae Regis* at an annual salary of £10,000. The Duke was by now hopelessly in debt, so this offer came as manna from heaven. But popular opinion had it that a son doing his duty to his father did not justify such a salary, and that four horses a week to travel from Frederick's house, the former royal palace at Oatlands in Surrey, to Windsor Castle should suffice.

Every Man has his Hobby Horse
ine is worth Ten Thousand !!!
To Windsor
Oatlands
f £ 10,000 Per Ann. by SAVING TRAVELLING EXPENCES.
s to WINDSOR as Appointed by ****** having only the small sum of Ten Thousand Pounds Per Year granted for
procured a Pedestrian Hobby Horse.
London pub. by Sidebothem. 287 Strand 1819

LE QOQUE EN PATE
Rowlandson

Public Transport

The Paris Diligence

Artist: Thomas Rowlandson
Published in 1810 by T. Tegg, 111 Cheapside

Thomas Rowlandson first went to France as a sixteen-year-old in 1772 to study drawing at the Académie Royal in Paris. Although this scene was published some forty years later, it shows a picturesque, pre-Revolutionary landscape. Thomas Tegg often reissued prints from old plates, and may have used an engraving made earlier by Rowlandson.

The picture is dominated by the Paris Diligence, or stage coach, which is leaving the yard of an inn, Le Qoque en Pate. The huge, lumbering coach is drawn by four rather skeletal horses driven by two postillions. In front is a massive basket, probably the luggage wagon. The main part of the coach is also made of basket-work, with open windows through which an assortment of passengers may be seen: friars (showing it is pre-Revolutionary France), peasant women, a veteran with a pigtail, a fashionable lady ogling a beau in a powdered wig. On top of the coach are two army officers with their female companion holding a parasol, and a girl with a fan who tries to flirt with a friar deep in his book. The coach is accompanied on its creaking, slow way by a group of beggars and a sow with her litter.

In the background can be seen a smarter, faster conveyance, a post chaise. Behind it rides a post-boy wearing 'milk churn' boots. These were a source of astonishment to English visitors: in 1783 Horatio Nelson, setting out from Calais for Paris, commented on 'the curious figure the postillions and their rats of horses made together'.

The stage coach, the principal form of public transport on land, offered a wonderful opportunity to observe humanity, as Rowlandson has shown. Wedged in firmly, knees and elbows creating a phalanx against the jolting of the carriage, passengers would spend many hours swapping stories, discussing ailments, exchanging recipes, and trying to sleep.

The Horrors of Revolution

Fashionable Movements – or the Stray Birds frightened out of France

Artist: George Cruikshank
Published 1823 by G. Humphrey,
St James's Street

Just as the Civil War caused bitter political, religious and social divisions in seventeenth-century England, so the French Revolution was to do likewise at the end of the eighteenth century. The immediate response of many was delight that the autocratic regime of Louis XVI had been overturned. Charles James Fox rejoiced 'How much the greatest event it is that ever happened in the world, and how much the best.' Others were not so sure, and there was widespread fear that social revolution could spread to Britain.

Although peace was restored in 1815 with the defeat of Napoleon at the Battle of Waterloo, the threat of war continued to haunt. This caricature by George Cruikshank refers to one such scare in 1823. Flocks of poultry, terrified by visions of revolutionary monsters in France, rush towards the Channel. On the right is a cock, emblem of Gallic unpredictability, on one of the windmills of Montmartre. A guillotine is surmounted by a scowling giant's head, wearing a red cap and shouting 'Fee-Faw-Fum – I smell the Blood of an Englishman'. Ironically, the scare was provoked by Louis XVIII, the French king

reinstalled by the British, intervening in Spain to secure the tyrannical Ferdinand VII on his throne, so renewed revolution was the least likely danger.

On the English side of the Channel, Britannia stands on the edge of the cliff, beckoning to the terrified creatures. Below her stands John Bull, a figure invented in 1712 who had become the representative of all that was regarded as basically British. A rhyme written in 1779 declared:

> 'With Porter, Roast Beef
> and Plumb Pudding
> well crammed
> Jack English declared
> that Monsieur may be
> damned.'

Here John Bull refers to ungenerous birds feeding on his grain and laying their golden eggs in other people's farmyards. He is alluding to the agricultural distress that would be alleviated if war were to come so that the price of bread might rise. The distress of the farmers, that is, but not of the unfortunate poor, who could starve.

Foreign ways

The Return from the Continent; or the Family puzzled

Artist: Phillips
Published 12 October 1827 by G. Humphrey, 24 St James's Street

Caricaturists often touched upon the love-hate relationship between Britain and France. The two nations were frequently at war through the eighteenth century, and for the first years of the nineteenth century. Horatio Nelson's injunction was that Britons 'must hate a Frenchman as the Devil'. Yet as soon as hostilities ceased, British tourists made their way to France to discover the latest fashions in style, food, and above all in dress.

In 1763, Tobias Smollett wrote 'When an Englishman comes to Paris, he cannot appear until he has undergone a total metamorphosis....The good man, who used to wear the *beau drap d'Angleterre*, quite plain all the year round, with a long bob or a tye periwig, must have provided himself with a camblet suit trimmed with silver for spring and autumn, with silk cloaths for summer, with cloth laced with gold or velvet for the winter; and he must wear his bag-wig à la pigeon'.

Nearly seventy years later, when this caricature was published, the fashions may have changed but the message was still the same. The lady of the house is so astonished by the return home of her large and rotund tradesman husband that she misses her cup with the teapot and pours it on the plate instead. He is shown in a burlesque of the latest French fashion, with a hat that looks remarkably like a traffic cone, a striped waistcoat and white trousers. She cries '... What, is that a French collar? why it sticks out like two large horns; and they've stuck a sugar-loaf on your head.... His reply, 'O! all a mode!' is echoed by their amused daughter, who warns her father, 'You'll have all the customers take you for a French Mounseer'. Behind the traveller are his caped greatcoat, portmanteau, and a souvenir of his journey, a poodle likewise clipped in French fashion, looking surprised and resentful.

Lord, my dear! the French folks have quite transmogrify'd you. What, is that a French collar? why, it sticks out like two large horns; — and they've stuck a sugar-loaf on your head — and what have they been doing with your small cloaths? — and where's your wig, my dear?

All a mode! all a mode! Why, papa you seem to have forgot all your English. You'll habe all the customers take you for a French Mounseer.

Pub. by G. Humphrey 24 St. James's St. Oct. 12, 1827.

A Price for Everything

The Four Mr Prices

Artist: George Cruikshank
Published 5 January 1825 by G. Humphrey, 24 St James's Street

After the title comes the explanation of this engraving: 'Four gentlemen of the Name of Price, all of very different dimensions, are thus distinguished by their friends. The Tall one, is called – High Price – the short one Low Price, the Fat one Full Price & the Thin one Half Price – Examiner'.

The identity of only one of these figures has been suggested. Stephen Price, Manager of the Drury Lane Theatre, was generally known as 'Half Price'. The custom of providing half-price tickets for the theatre was introduced in the early eighteenth century, when John Rich, who managed the theatres in Lincoln's Inn Fields and Covent Garden, offered an afterpiece to follow the main play. This would consist of a pantomime or a short farce, and proved so popular that when the Patent Theatres (those that had the royal or official patent) threatened to abolish the concession, riots broke out.